Automotive Computer Network Repair

(Diagnostic Strategies of Modern Automotive Systems)

By Mandy Concepcion

Copyright © 2006, 2011 By Mandy Concepcion

This book is copyrighted under Federal Law to prevent the unauthorized use or copying of its contents. Under copyright law, no part of this work can be reproduced, copied or transmitted in any way or form without the written permission of its author, Mandy Concepcion.

Copyright © 2006, 2011 By Mandy Concepcion

Preface

In this book we will cover the intricacies of automotive inter-module communication systems or networks. The scope of this section will also go beyond the normal needs of an automotive technician. Hence, this will probably be the most difficult part of this series to comprehend. Be patient and open minded. Always give yourself time to absorb the knowledge and do not be discouraged. Special emphasis will be placed on the CAN system (Controller Area Network), since it is now the standard.

CAN is one of the 9 OBD-2 protocols. A protocol is an agreement on communications interchange. It is in essence a computer communication language and specifies signaling, wiring, size of cables used, who controls the network and voltage levels. Various protocols were used in the past, some proprietary and some generic such as ISO 9141 and SAE 1850 VPW, but the standard is now the CAN protocol.

Virtually all vehicle networks now talk to each other though the CAN protocol. It is now common place to see the seat belt, SRS-Airbag, transmission, ABS-Brakes, engine and radio modules or computer talking to each other through the network. Ever wondered why your radio volume goes up when you accelerate the vehicle? That's the engine computer or module telling the radio to raise the volume due to a higher RPM and hence higher ambient noise. It is also common to see a non-shifting transmission due to a faulty network and the issue not being related to the transmission at all. Hopefully this book will shed some light on the operation and knowledge needed to tackle automotive networks in today's vehicles...... Enjoy.

Automotive Computer Network Repair (Section 8)

Table of Contents

1. INTRODUCTION

* - Automotive inter-module communication systems or networks

* - Asian, Domestics and European Vehicles

* - Fully Networked vehicles.

2. THE NEED FOR IN-VEHICLE NETWORKING

* - Use of electrical and electronic components

* - Networked automotive sensors.

* - Sharing of sensor information

* - Weight savings and the simpler wiring harnesses

* - Networking and modular systems

3. THE NEED FOR PROTOCOLS

* - **CAN** or Controller Area Network communication protocol

* - **CLASS A** – Low speed

* - **CLASS B** – Medium speed

* - **CLASS C** – High speed

* - **SAE** (Society of Automotive Engineers)

* - **ISO** (International Standards Organization)

* - What is a Gateway?

4. NETWORKING ESSENTIALS

* - the 7-layer ISO/OSI reference model

* - PHYSICAL LAYER

* - DATA LINK LAYER

* - APPLICATION LAYER

* - The Node Oriented and Message Oriented (Producer-Consumer) protocols

* - Medium Access

* - CARRIER SENSE MULTIPLE ACCESS or CSMA

* - Network latency

* - The Topology of a network

* - The STAR topology

* - The BUS topology

* - The TREE topology

* - The RING topology

5. DIFFERENT COMMUNICATION NETWORK

* - The CCD data bus (Chrysler Collision Detection)

* - CCD bus ground

* - CCD bus bias voltage

* - OEM scan tool (DRB III)

* - NO TERMINATION message fault

* - The PCI bus (Programmable Communications Interface)

* - A CSMA/CD media access scheme

* - The Header, DATA, CRC, IFR and EOF elements

* - DCL (Data Communications Link)

* - circuit 914 and 915

* - SCP (J1850) (Standard Corporate Protocol)

* - Dual wire twisted pair bus topology

* - The ISO 9141 protocol

* - The NGS "DATA LINK DIAGNOSTICS" menu option

* - GM (Data Line) UART Serial Communications

* - UART data line communications

* - GM CLASS 2 data bus

* - State of health messages

* - The Tech-2 scanner has a dynamic menu configuration

* - The Tech-2's PING-ALL-MODULES

6. CAN (Controller Area Network)

* - implementation of the CAN protocol

* - 11 bit and 29 bit identifyer

* - EPA approved for MY 2003 and up

* - CAN A, B and C

* - MID and PID CAN identifyers

* - Master time-keeper-node

* - Drive-by-wire systems

* - Byteflight, Flexray, and Time-triggered CAN or TTCAN

* - The CAN Data-Frame

* - Recessive (high) or dominant (low) CAN communication.

* - The CAN bus-access arbitration

* - SOF (start-of-frame) bit

* - Control bit

* - Arbitration bits

* - Data bits

* - EOF or end of frame bit

VEHICLE NETWORKS

(AUTOMOTIVE COMMUNICATION SYSTEMS REPAIR STRATEGY)

1. INTRODUCTION.

In this article, we will cover the intricacies of automotive inter-module communication systems or networks. The scope of this section will also go beyond the normal needs of an automotive technician. Hence, this will probably be the most difficult part of this book to comprehend. Be patient and open minded. Always give yourself time to absorb the knowledge and do not be discouraged. Special emphasis will be placed on CAN systems (Controller Area Network). CAN technology, as used today in automobiles, is becoming the standard in vehicle networking and the need for a sound understanding of this technology is fundamental. However, as CAN networks exists today, it is probably not necessary to go into such an in-depth study like will be doing so in here. But, there is a trend towards a totally networked vehicle. By that we mean networking not only the different modules but every single sensor and actuator found in a vehicle. This implementation of networking technology will require a deep understanding of protocols and networking in general. With this in mind, extra time has been devoted to thoroughly cover the details of the CAN system. Future automotive technicians will work on vehicles where all the different networked sensors and actuators no longer put out an analog signal. Such components output a digital network signal and can not be tested with a common multimeter.

This is already happening on some Asian and European automobiles, whereby, important sensors are already being networked. A good example is the steering angle sensor and Nissans power window switches. In these cases, the networked sensors will output a digital signal or what is called a network data frame. Only another controller running on the same network can understand that signal. As of right now, few sensors are fully networked but, as the amount of sensors keeps growing the need to network them becomes apparent. And, the same holds true for actuators as well. Because of the savings in weight and less complex wiring harnesses, sensor and actuator networking becomes very attractive. So, with this in mind and an eye towards the future, lets broaden our knowledge. Your learning sacrifice now will pay off later. Remember when someone compliments you in the future on how good of a tech you are, simply tell them – "Well is either ass, gas or grass but everybody absolutely everybody has to pay."

See our complimentary DVD-Video series for this book.

2. THE NEED FOR IN-VEHICLE NETWORKING.

Today's modern automobiles make use of electrical and electronic components like never before. Gone are the days when a vehicle's fuse box was the most complicated component the car had. The issue of complexity as well as weigh has already become a major problem. It is estimated that today's luxury vehicles carry as much as 3 miles of wires at nearly 250 lbs. It is also normal to see many of the safety and convenience items on today's mid-range vehicles that where found only on luxury makes of years past. And this technology will trickle down to the most basic models in the coming years. Which only means that the amount and complexity of future automotive electronics will swell. Due of the complexity as well as extra weight savings, vehicle manufacturers have had, and will even more so in the future, invested on sophisticated in-vehicle communications systems. And this only means NETWORKING! Automotive communication networks make it easy to accomplish more with less. With smaller and fewer components and wiring, more can be done. The tremendous savings in the way systems can be put together, due to the modular nature of networks, is also a major advantage. And not to mention the use of simpler and easy to install wiring harnesses. Traditionally automobile manufacturers have used the old point-to-point-wiring scheme. In this case, the different sensors and actuators in a vehicle are hard wired to their applicable module. This practice has worked fine, with the small quantity of automotive components in the past. However, because of the increased in wiring necessary for newer and future vehicle systems, the trend has been to use inter-module networks to accomplish more with less wiring. By simply making all the different modules in a vehicle talk to each other, a tremendous amount of weight savings can be achieved.

For example:

Most manufacturers use the TPS to indicate to the engine module, the transmission module and in some cases the ABS module as to what the throttle opening/rate of change is. All these modules need the TPS signal to operate. If we were to use the old style wiring scheme (point-to-point), the TPS signal wire will have to split to each of these mentioned modules. Multiplied by all the different sensors and actuators on a vehicle, the amount of wiring and extra weight is staggering. However, by simply using a one or two wire communications network, the information from the TPS as well as all the sensors and actuators in the vehicle can be shared. Imagine the vehicle network as an inter-module phone line.

The networked phone line is connected to all the modules in the vehicle and with it, all the sensor/actuator information is shared. So long as the sensor or actuator in question is connected to just one networked module, its information will be transmitted and shared by all connected applicable modules. All this signaling information is simply put out on the network and used by the module that needs it. A power door lock module for example does not need a TPS signal, therefore, the power door lock controller will ignore this signal information. With that in mind, we will look at some of the benefits of modern networks.

• The first benefit of vehicle networking is the sharing of sensor information. By simply eliminating the need for many redundant sensors and related wiring, the system can be made simpler. Why have two TPS sensors? The same can be said for actuators. By simply networking the different actuators in a vehicle, a simple command issued by one of the modules is enough to trigger it into action.

• A second benefit of networking is the weight savings and the simpler wiring harnesses. This alone would make the vehicle more fuel efficient and cheaper to make. Automotive wiring harnesses are very expensive to make and to maintain.

Finally an even greater advantage to this technology is the modular nature of it. By that we mean, that by simply adding another module and connecting it to the network a new system can be brought to production. Networking in this case makes the task of having to hot wire a new system (point-to-point wiring) unnecessary. An example is the use of traction control systems on newer vehicles. All the manufacturer has to do is add a new Traction Control module that works in conjunction with the ABS, ECM and Trans module and this system becomes a reality. With traction control systems, none or very little actual hardware is actually used. The traction control module uses the existing modules (ABS, ECM and TCM) to add that higher level of safety to the vehicle. And of course, the manufacturers charge dearly for it. The recent addition of an array of new features like stability control, adaptive suspension, memory profile system (driver's handling preference), etc are all possible because of vehicle networking. And this is only the beginning of a trend that will continue for years to come.

NOTE: Notice the term above "signal information". In a networked system the signals are no longer analog. In other words, a TPS signal will not look like a changing voltage signal on the oscilloscope. In order to transmit any signal output from a sensor on the network, it will have to be converted into a digital signal by the connected module. Then the particular module sends this digital signal over the network inside a DATA FRAME, which we'll go into later.

See our complimentary DVD-Video series for this book.

3. THE NEED FOR PROTOCOLS

As vehicle networking becomes more commonplace, the need for a standardized protocol has become an issue. Enter CAN or Controller Area Network communication protocol to the scene. A protocol is nothing more than an agreement on information interchange. A protocol is NOT a physical component nor is it a program or software. In simple terms, a protocol is a set of rules that simply say 2 beeps is a letter A, 3 beeps is a letter B and so on. The CAN protocol or a derivative of it is becoming the de-facto standard in the automotive industry. CAN was developed by the Robert Bosch Corporation in the early 1980's specifically for the automotive industry. But it is by no means the only network protocol in use today. This article will study the different protocols found today, as well as their differences. However, emphasis will be placed on the CAN protocol, since it is destined to be the standard. But first a word about networks in general. All in-vehicle communication network is divided into three general classifications.

● **CLASS A** – Low speed – less than 10K bits/second. (This type of network is used for entertainment features, radio, CD control, lighting, etc.)

● **CLASS B** – Medium speed – between 10K bits/second to 125K bits/second. (This type is used for semi-critical information exchange like instrument cluster, vehicle speed, diagnostics scanner, emission data exchange, etc.)

● **CLASS C** – High speed – between 125K bits/second to 1 Megabit/sec. (Real-time communications. Used for engine control, drive-by-wire, brake-by-wire, etc.) It is said that Class C if used for scanner communications, would be like using an oscilloscope, because of the speed of transmission.

There are two standardization agencies that govern the automotive world. In the US is SAE (Society of Automotive Engineers) and it has the responsibility of setting all the standards for automobiles, as well as other industries as well. The rest of the world uses ISO (International Standards Organization) based in France and it dictates the automotive standards for Europe and the rest of the automobile producing countries. SAE defined these three vehicle network classifications based on speed. Class A being the slowest to Class C the fastest. When engineers design vehicle networks, due to the direct impact on the cost of the vehicle, always take the SAE classification system into account.

There is no sense in using a Class C network for convenience gadgets. Class C uses very expensive electronic components, which rises the cost of the modules used in the vehicle. This is why it is common to find a Class A or B and a Class C working simultaneously in the same vehicle. It just saves money.

NOTE: Different class networks (different speeds) can be found working together, but divided by a device called a GATEWAY. A gateway simply acts as a translator between two unequal networks. The gateway circuitry is normally embedded inside another module, like the instrument cluster module, for example. In this case, if the instrument cluster module fails, so does the gateway circuit. This will bring down half or even the entire network.

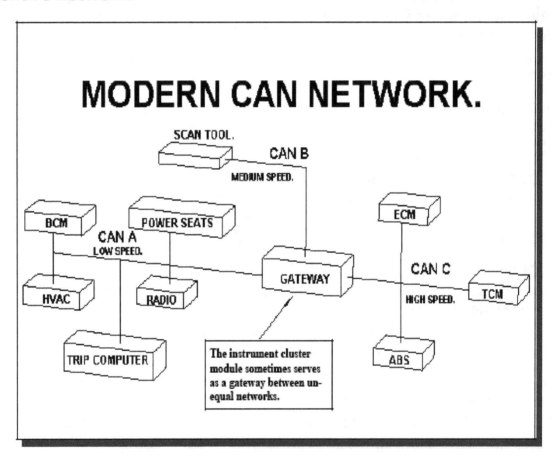

Fig 1 – A gateway is used to connect different class networks.

A number of vehicles today use two or even three separate networks, linked by gateway. In this arrangement the slower (Class A) convenience network (Radio, memory seat, trip computer, power windows/locks, etc) can co-exist and communicate with the fastest (Class C) real-time critical network (engine, ABS, TCM, X-by-wire systems) via a gateway. This makes it possible for the two systems to share information. An example of this is a feature found on some factory radios, whereby the volume is raised automatically when the driver accelerates to make up for the louder engine noise. Such level of integration is made possible by the ability of these two unequal networks to communicate.

CLASS A (Low speed, UART)

The first Class A network protocols utilized inexpensive communications circuitry such as UART. UART (Universal Asynchronous Receive and Transmit) technology was widely implemented by GM and others in early systems going back to the 1980's. However, UART protocols were not standardized and therefore utilized proprietary technology that no one else knew but the manufacturer. This is also the reason why some of the first after-market scan tools started to appear almost a decade after the first UART systems came on the market. The proprietary UART protocols simply had to be decoded or backward engineered and that took time. It is possible to see UART networks even today, but only for low speed applications as in seat control modules, power windows/locks, etc. UART or any other Class A network can also be linked to a higher speed (Class B or C) network by means of a gateway circuit.

CLASS B (Medium speed, GM class 2, SCP, SAE J1850, CAN B)

The Class B network is widely used today and is the most used classification for vehicle communications. This type of network is used for everything from sensor sharing, body controllers, instrument clusters to diagnostics tools. However it is not a real-time network, hence is not fast enough to be used in late model X-by-wire systems. The X-by-wire designation is the general term for all the electronically controlled systems (brake-by-wire, drive-by-wire, steer-by-wire, etc). GM adopted a Class B type network, which they renamed Class 2. GM's Class 2 is a medium speed communications network, which is in current use today. It is used on most GM models and will eventually be replaced by a derivative of the CAN protocol or GM's interpretation of it (GM LAN). It is also important to know that the CAN protocol can also be implemented in a Class B network. The protocol is just the agreement on information inter-change and the classification is simply how fast the network is. The faster the network, the more expensive it is. FORD also adopted the Class B network, which they named SCP (FORD Standard Corporate Protocol). CHRYSLER implementation of the Class B network is called CCD bus (Chrysler Collision Detection) and PCI bus (programmable communications interface).

CARB (California Air Resources Board) early on adopted a Class B network called SAE J1850. This is now the basis for all OBD II systems. The J1850 protocol was a joint effort from GM and FORD. It is a derivative of the CLASS 2 and SCP protocols. A somewhat similar OBD II protocol (J1850) in Europe is the ISO 9141-2/14230.

CLASS C (High speed, real-time, CAN)

The main CLASS C protocol for automotive use to date is CAN 2.0. The CAN protocol was developed in the early 1980's by the Robert Bosch Corporation and was created, specifically for automotive use. It is also used today for industrial applications, including automation. This protocol has true high-speed applications, being able to operate as high as 1 Meg bit/sec. Although, because of automotive peripheral problems (possible interference), it is used at no higher than 500 K bit/sec. The CAN protocol is also a true real-time network protocol, which means that the data travels with few detectable delays. In other words, the data rate looks more like a multi-meter or an oscilloscope. In diagnostics applications, this means that the actual PID data scan looks more like true real life readings than the more commonly found delayed scanner readings. There is one important factor to understand about scanners and CAN and it is that although the CAN protocol is many times faster than anything in wide use today, this factor has nothing to do with the scan tool's screen refresh rate. What it means is that if the manufacturer decides that it is not necessary for the technician to have a fast refresh data rate, the scan tool will simply be slower than the actual network speed. There are a couple of reasons for this to happen. One is the old higher cost, bottom line dilemma and the other is that it might not be sensible to put a fast acting scan tool data for that particular application. There is no need for a high refresh data rate for body applications for example or to read an O2 sensor. These PIDs require a slower data rate with no need for faster, more expensive electronics. Another possibility is the technician chasing unnecessary fast acting glitches that are normal, thus increasing the manufacturer's warranty service expense.

See our complimentary DVD-Video series for this book.

4. NETWORKING ESSENTIALS

All modern networks are based on the ISO/OSI Reference Model (International Standards Organization). This model is also known as the 7-layer ISO/OSI reference model, because on paper it is actually composed of seven hierarchical imaginary representative layers. Each of these layers actually represents a specific level of need for information interchange. The data passes through the layers and as it does, bits of information are added on to it. For example, a stream of data being transmitted has to get disassembled, encoded and sent over the network lines or data bus. After the data is received at the receiving node (module, actuator, etc) it has to get decoded, reassembled and then put together with the rest of the incoming data to be used properly. All this data manipulation takes extra bits of information to be able to get put back together properly. Every time the data passes through a control layer, the protocol (through the software) adds these extra bits of control information. Error detection and handling is also the domain of these protocol layer stacks and again, extra bits of information are added to manage the error control properly. Being that the OSI model was intended for any type of communication system, some systems may not use all of the 7 layers of the OSI model. In CAN only 3 layers are used, which are the PHYSICAL LAYER, DATA LINK LAYER and APPLICATION LAYER.

These three layers are only relevant in automotive applications. The apparent limitations of only using 3 layers actually increases the efficiency of the protocol stack and reduces the latency time (delay time) of the network. This is due to the reduced amount of layers that the software has to deal with.

Physical Layer – This layer encompasses the electrical, encoding and functional characteristics of the protocol stack. Thus, this layer is in charge of encoding the data into a stream of bits so as to be able to send it over the network lines. On the receiver end, this layer is in charge of decoding the transmitted bits into the original data that was sent. The reassembled data is then prepared to be passed-on to the Data link layer. Everything related to bit timing and bit synchronization as well as the actual physical connection (cables) to the network is the responsibility of this layer.

Data Link Layer – The second layer of the protocol stack makes possible the transmission of data between nodes. This involves the assembly of the data frames, which is the center of any network transmission sequence. The frames also contain not just the data but control information, as well as error handling and detection bits.

The control bits are needed to put all this back together. They simply instruct the node on how to extract and reassemble the data from the physical layer. The error detection bits are put into the frame and sent along so that the receiving end can view them and detect any missing bits. If any error bits are missing it would constitute an error and re-transmission of the data would be necessary. The sender automatically retransmits the defective or erroneous data frame once detected from the error detection bits. A second function of the data link layer is the control of the network access by a node or module. In other words, when two or more nodes try and access the network at the same time this layer simply resolves the problem and no data is lost.

Application Layer – The application layer actually carries and handles the codes and functions related to the software. All program code use this layer to perform its operation. Such functions as file transfer and code execution are its domain. Whether accessing part of an imbedded program or performing a module re-programming (re-flashing) the application layer handles all the details.

The Node Oriented and Message Oriented (Producer-Consumer) protocols are the two main types of data communication system protocols. Communication systems whereby the data is broadcast over the network to all that want to listen are synonymous of the producer-consumer type. The data broadcast by the producer (transmitter) over the network can either be consumed (received) or be ignored. This is the model followed by the CAN protocol. The node or module that wants to transmit data (steering angle sensor, Body Control Module or ECM) simply does so without it being requested to do so. For example, it is simply programmed into the system that the ECM should transmit a TPS signal every so often and the receiving module does NOT have to ask for it. Automobiles use this category of protocol exclusively today. This type of protocol is also called a message identifier based system. The data frame transmitted by a specific node or module has its identifier bits in it. The destination of this data frame is never defined. It is simply the decision of all receiving node (s) to either accept or reject the data. In a message-oriented protocol, the transmitter does not know or cares who the receiver is. It just transmits.

On the other hand, a node-oriented protocol would have the modules send the data stream with their own node (module) identification, and no node (module) can transmit data unless requested to do so. Therefore, the exchange of data using this type of protocol is based on node or module addressing. With node-oriented the data frames have both, the node's address (identification) and the target address (where it's going). Simply put, a data message is sent to a specific node only and hence the name node-oriented. Almost all conventional (business & industrial) communication systems use this protocol model.

Medium Access is the ability of a network protocol to regulate or judge which transmitting node gains access to the transmission medium (network lines). If two or more nodes try to access the network at the same time, the protocol has to be able to decide who gets to go first. Medium access control actually prevents multiple nodes from accessing the network at the same time, by way of message identifier arbitration (CAN protocol). Otherwise, these multiple node transmissions would interfere with each other freezing the network completely.

In network communications there are two main methods of medium access. These are determined access and random access. In determined access, the bus (network lines) is accessed through a main master node or by way of token passing. In the first method, a master synchronization node gives each node the permission to access the network. The drawback in this type of access method is that if the master node goes bad, so does the rest of the network. The second deter mined access method is the token passing system. In token passing, a chance or network access permission is passed along the network from node to node. If the node that has the access permission or token wants to transmit data, it can do so at that time. Once the token passes to another node that previous node looses the chance to transmit until the next time around when the token is received again. This method rules out transmission collisions and guaranties that only one node can access the network at a time. These systems are not used in CAN or in automobiles in general. For CAN we go to the random access medium access methods. In random access the nodes can access the network as soon as the bus is idle.

Therefore, the nodes are always listening for network activity and will transmit as soon as they detect no activity. This is called CARRIER SENSE MULTIPLE ACCESS or CSMA. These two methods can be further divided into CSMA with collisions and without collisions. CSMA/CD (collision detection) access methods simply has a way to detect such collision and correct them without data loss. On the other hand, CSMA/CA (collision avoidance) simply avoids these collisions altogether. This is done by way of identifier arbitration. In other words, the identifier with the highest priority gets to access the network first. The CAN protocol is a full CSMA/CA medium access system. This access method lowers the latency time for high priority nodes so that if an SAS (steering angle sensor), throttle control module or a vehicle accelerometer wants to access the network, it always gets priority. All these sensors may use high prioritymessages.

NOTE: Latency refers to the amount of time that a node (module, actuator or controller) has to wait for the network to free up. With the CAN protocol only using 3 layers, each node is able to transmit and receive information faster.

The sensor or node simply has to wait until the presently occurring transmission ends and the bus goes idle in order to transmit. An idle bus simply means that the nodes can transmit as soon as they want to. If other lower priority nodes access the bus at the same time, the high priority node will win access regardless. This is why this access method lends itself to automotive use so readily, being that higher priority (higher priority identifier) nodes have higher access provisions under the CSMA/CA protocol.

The Topology of a network describes the physical connections between all the nodes in the network. The network topology is the main determinant of how expensive and/or limited a particular network will be. The main network topologies are the star, bus, ring and the tree topology.

• **The STAR topology**, as the name implies, has all the nodes connected in a star configuration. This is the simplest topology. The nodes are actually connected to a central node. Each node being connected directly to this central node. It is an easily expandable network, with any future node being directly connected to the central node. The disadvantages to this topology is more wiring necessary to connect each node, in case of a large amount of nodes the central node requires an excessive amount of connections, communications are only possible through the central node and if it fails the entire network fails. This situation however can be remedied by the use of a multi-star topology. In this case, the central node gives birth to other central nodes and a bigger, more fault tolerant network topology can be built. The multi-star topology is used today in automobiles.

• **The BUS topology** has all the nodes connected to a common medium or wire and the data transmitted is available to all nodes. This arrangement uses less cabling and simpler connections. Adding more nodes to the bus is done by simply taping into the bus (wiring) and failure of one node does not affect the other nodes. The disadvantages are that signal regeneration (repeaters) are needed for long networks, both ends of the bus cables have to be terminated by a terminating resistor, and node identification is generally required. A terminating resistor is used in order to avoid signal reflections.

The value of the terminating resistor has to be chosen according to the line impedance and in CAN applications it is usually about 120 Ohms. The failure of the terminating resistor is the main cause for the loss of the network bias voltage. The loss of network bias will cause a multiple module communications failure. Chrysler's scanner, the DRB III, has a menu option to bias the network whenever the bias voltage is lost, due to a faulty terminating resistor. After biasing the network with the DRB III, communications with all the modules can be regained and diagnostics can be carried out to determine the root cause of the problem. This topology is by far the most widely used on automotive networks. The bus topology should not be confused with the data bus definition. In general a data bus is any cabling arrangement where communications take place.

• **The TREE topology** is a combination of the star and bus topology. This arrangement is highly flexible but can become too costly. It has few automotive applications.

• The RING topology is a node-to-node connection arrangement. Its main advantage is signal regeneration because the transmission passes from node to node. Each time the transmission goes to the next node, it gets amplified. This topology is widely used in automotive entertainment fiber optics networks. The Digital Data Bus (D2B) system is a fiber optics network used widely on European vehicles, which uses the ring topology. It is capable of achieving very high data rates.

The general requirements of the network dictate which topology to use. A low cost application will probably dictate a bus type topology as well as cheaper electronics—while a high-speed D2B fiber optics entertainment network will be the ring type and much more expensive to implement. The high cost associated with the electronic components is the main reason why manufacturers do not simply go with a super-fast fiber optic system right now. The old bottom line dictates the course of action. But, as network chip technology gets cheaper, these faster networks will find their way to the lower end models and to the mass market in general.

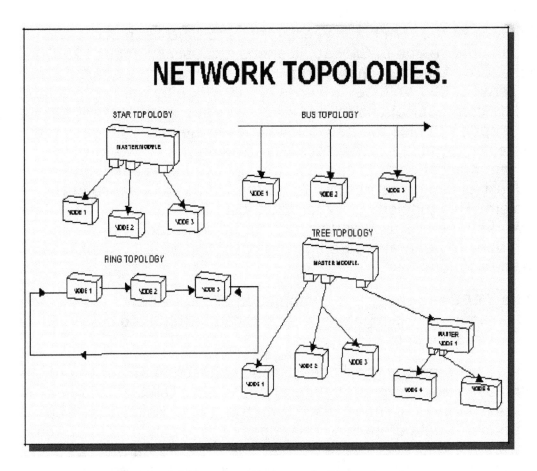

Fig-2. Different Network Topologies.

See our complimentary DVD-Video series for this book.

5. DIFFERENT MANUFACTURERS' COMMUNICATIONS NETWORK

CHRYSLER

The CCD data bus (Chrysler Collision Detection) In the early 90's, Chrysler came up with a new and very advanced vehicle communications network protocol. They called it CCD (Chrysler Collision Detection), with a network speed of 7.81 K bits/Sec. The CCD network uses a bus topology configuration. A dual twisted pair wires runs to all the modules, which makes for a less expensive network to implement. In latter model years, the CCD bus was implemented using a star configuration, with the BCM as a central master node. The CCD protocol is message oriented and somewhat similar to the CAN protocol, which was already in use in Europe at that time. It also uses priority identifier media access arbitration or the ability to give a higher priority node/module a high access based on its level of importance. The two twisted wires that make up the data bus are called D1 (bus +) and D2 (bus −) respectively. Each of the wires carries a bias voltage level of 2.50 volts dc with respect to network ground. In this case D1 (bus +) is 2.50 volts dc with respect to network ground and D2 (bus -) is −2.50 volts dc with respect to network ground. It is good to pint out that the CCD bus ground is a floating ground and not the vehicle's battery ground. Together both D1 and D2 have a total bias voltage of 5.00 volts across each other. By pulling the bias voltage low the communications bits are created for inter-module communications, which means that an idle CCD bus (no communications) has a level of 2.50 volts with respect to battery ground. The D1 and the D2 lines toggle in opposite direction to each other. This arrangement is called differential signaling and it is used for error detection and redundancy.

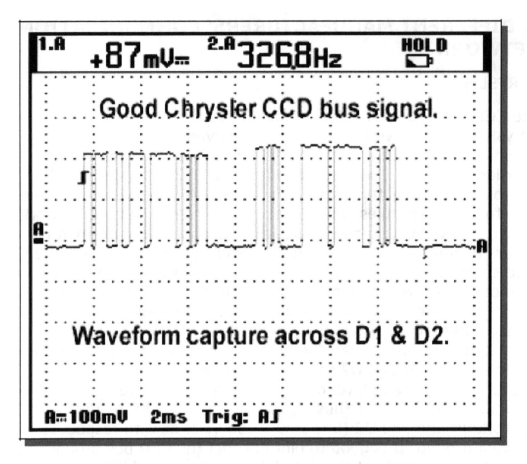

Fig-3. Signal waveform capture of a Chrysler CCD signal.

NOTE: In order to be able to capture a network waveform, it is necessary to probe across the D1 and D2 terminals. The battery ground should not be used as a reference ground

Certain designated modules in the network provide the CCD bus bias voltage, as well as having a resistor voltage divider network. In order to produce the bias voltage, a resistor voltage divider network is needed. This voltage divider resistor network is imbedded inside the biasing module (s). Termination resistors are also needed for proper CCD bus operation and besides the fact that they provide a sink for the bias voltage, they also protect against electromagnetic interference. Termination resistor value is usually about 120 ohms. At least one termination resistor is needed in the network. Therefore, a CCD bus system has some modules with bias/voltage divider network and some with termination resistors. Certain modules, like the BCM, are also able to provide both bias voltage and termination resistance at the same time. Without a termination resistor, the bus voltage would jump to 5.00 volts on one wire and 0.00 volts on the other.

NOTE: It is important to know that Chrysler's OEM scan tool (DRB III) can provide the bus with the + and − 2.50 volts (5.00 volts total) needed in the event that the network bias voltage goes down. This is very useful for CCD network diagnostics. A loss of the bias voltage will bring the network down, since each module communicates by grounding the bias voltage. In many cases, by providing the network bias voltage with the scanner, communications can be reestablished.

The following modules exchange information through the CCD bus. This list however is not limited.

• Body Control Module (BCM).

• Transmission Control Module (EATX).

• Mechanical Instrument Cluster (MIC).

• Powertrain Control Module (PCM/ECM).

• Air Bag Module (SRS/ACM/AECM/ASDM/DAB).

• Overhead Travel Information System (OTIS).

• Anti Lock Brakes (ABS).

• Automatic Temp. Control (ATC) if equipped.

• Remote Keyless Entry (RKE).

• Vehicle Theft Security System (VTSS).

The BCM and the PCM are normally providers of bias and voltage divider resistors. The resistor network is imbedded inside each module's PC board and without it there is no bias voltage. One of the first things to check for in the absence of bias voltage is the two-pin CCD output from the BCM and PCM. A 120-ohm resistance value should be observed.

NOTE: Whenever experiencing a NO TERMINATION message fault with the DRB III connected, check the DRB III cable. The DRB III is capable of providing bias voltage as well as termination resistance. This means the as far as the CCD network is concerned, the DRB III is another module.

The CCD system relies on the inter-module message system of communication. Each module on the network acknowledges its presence on the network.

Any module that fails to acknowledge its presence is presumed faulty or having defective power and ground circuits. When this happen, a faulty code is stored in some of the other module's diagnostic memory. The location of the faulty code or message is already a diagnostic clue, since multiple modules usually expect a message from the faulty module. An example would be an inoperative TCM, which would cause a NO TCM MESSAGE code on the PCM and the BCM. By concentrating on the TCM circuitry, a decision can be reached as to what is the cause of the communications problem such as the actual CCD bus, power or ground circuits. The CCD protocol is also a broadcast type system like the CAN protocol. Messages and data are transmitted to all modules on the network. It is up to each particular module to either accept or reject the information.

The PCI bus (Programmable Communications Interface)

In 1997 Chrysler introduced yet another communications protocol. They called it PCI or programmable communications interface, with a network speed of 10.8 K bit/Sec. The PCI bus consists of a single (20-gage) wire network arranged in a star configuration. Chrysler calls this circuit D25 and is usually labeled violet/yellow. PCI uses Variable Pulse Width Modulation signaling for communications, which differs from the previous CCD system. The BCM usually serves as the central master node and controls all the network traffic. The modules on the PCI bus also use local grounds as their bus ground reference. Hence the use of only a single wire for communication signaling.

The PCI bus follows a message arbitration scheme somewhat similar to the CCD system. Termination resistors and capacitors are needed with this system but this system uses NO bias voltage for communications. Each communicating module simply provides or switches the network voltage ON and OFF by means of internal transceiver drivers. The PCI bus uses a 7.50 volts value for its high (active) and 0.00 volts (ground) for its low (passive) signals. However a high signal state does not mean a binary 1 nor does a low signal state means a binary 0. This type of signaling is used in order to minimize errors as mush as possible. The binary encoding is in the variable pulse width nature of the signal. A communications waveform of this system would look like a square wave toggling between ground and 7.50 volts at a varying pulse width.

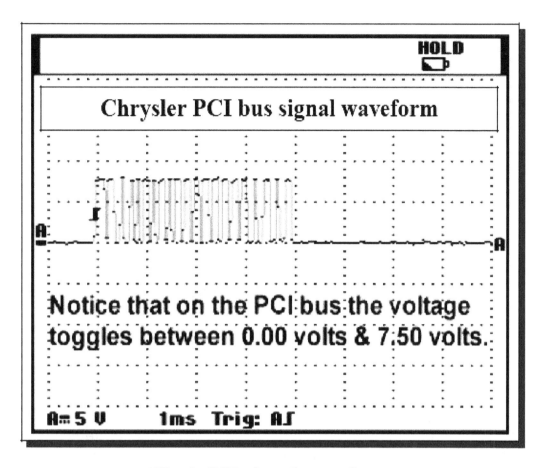

Fig 4. PCI signal waveform.

Termination resistance and capacitance are of absolute importance to this system, which can become unstable if these values are disturbed. Each module on the bus can only provide a current. The termination load resistance should be between 320 ohms - 2 k ohms and bus capacitance in the order of 10 pf. The bus internal resistance and capacitance is required to provide EMF protection and signal loading. Each module on the PCI bus has a small resistor and capacitor inside its internal PC board. These values are taken into account in the overall values of the termination load. However, one of the modules in the network carries a higher load or higher resistance value. This module is called the dominant module and is usually the PCM or the BCM.

A CSMA/CD media access scheme is used on the PCI bus as well as an identifier type priority arbitration. When a collision is detected, the node with lesser priority stops transmitting. In a PCI bus, the data frame is called the symbol or a message. Through the exchange of symbols all the modules are able to communicate with each other. A typical message is composed of 4 main elements.

• The header contains control bits like message length, priority, sending and destination node addresses.

• The data bytes are the actual data bits.

• The CRC error detection bits.

• The IFR (in-frame-response-bits) tell the receiving module if a response or additional data is needed.

• The EOF (end-of-frame) bits signaling the end of the message.

Through this type of frame arrangement, each PCI module can send and request additional data faster than otherwise. For example, if a TCM module needs an RPM signal right away and wants to send a VSS signal, it simply sends a frame to the PCM encoding the VSS signal and requesting the RPM signal at the same time. PCI is still in use today, but will soon be replaced by the CAN protocol, which is already the communications protocol for some Dodge trucks.

FORD DCL (Data Communications Link)

In the late 1980's FORD Motor Company started the first implementation of a proprietary network on their Lincoln vehicles. They called it DCL (Data Communications Link). The system used a proprietary protocol, which included the ECM (EEC IV), MCCA (Message Center Control Assembly), CCA (Cluster Control Assembly) and the diagnostics scanner. The system had a basic bus type topology, allowing it to share various signals over the network lines. The DCL uses a two wire bus labeled circuit 914 DCL (+) and circuit 915 DCL (-). The ECM transmitted the following signals over the DCL network:

• RPM, ECT, Check Engine Light, Fuel used. The CCA (instrument cluster) transmitted the following signals.

• Fuel level, Odometer, VSS, Display temperature, Battery voltage, Oil pressure, Temperature hot warning and low charge warning.

NOTE: Ford uses the terminology "circuit 914 and 915" to identify their network bus positive and negative leads. The company also uses "circuit 70" to identify their single wire ISO 9141 bus lead, which usually links the airbag and other systems.

The ECM broadcast the state of the check engine light over the network. In the event of a malfunction, the ECM will instruct the CCA to turn on the check engine light. The system was primitive by today's standards. In case of a network fault, the message light CHECK DCL would light up on the dash and the ECM would store a code 529/533 in memory indicating a network (DCL) circuit fault. Code 529 indicated an ECM network circuit fault and 533 a DCL to Instrument cluster circuit failure. The two major faulty areas were the CCA (instrument cluster) and the ECM itself. It was up to the technician to manually test the electronic circuits to verify the root of the problem.

SCP (J1850) (Standard Corporate Protocol)

In 1995 FORD released a new network protocol which was named SCP (Standard Corporate Protocol). The SCP protocol is based on a dual wire twisted pair bus topology. The system allowed different modules to communicate via circuit 914-BUS (+) and circuit 915-BUS (-). Pins 2 (BUS +) and 10 (BUS -) on the DLC are used for SCP communications. After 1996 the SCP protocol became OBD II (J1850) compliant. If one of the twisted pair wires failed (shorted, open, etc) the system can operate on the other wire and can also operate if one of the wires become shorted to ground or battery power. Either of these conditions will set a diagnostic trouble code.

NOTE: FORD separates the SRS (airbag) and some other modules on a different communications network and protocol. The ISO 9141 protocol (circuit 70/DLC pin 7) is used for SRS communications. This protocol also uses a single wire for communications. The ISO 9141 communications network does not allow inter-module communications initialization. For diagnostics, the scanner has to initiate the actual query of all the modules present.

The diagnosis of FORD communications network problems rely on the use of the NGS scan tool. The NGS "DATA LINK DIAGNOSTICS" menu option is very useful. This option queries all the modules for a presence response. Any module that does not respond is presumed faulty, pointing the technician in the right diagnostic direction. A deeper pinpoint test is then performed.

GM (Data Line) UART Serial Communications

In the late 1080's GM came up with their first inter-module communications system. The early systems used UART (Universal Asynchronous Receive and Transmit) communications chips, which were cheaper and easy to implement at the time.

These systems were proprietary in nature and never became standardized, not even within GM itself. NOTE: GM would usually call the data line circuit "circuit 800". These early systems were called UART data line communications and used a single wire in a ring or bus topology configuration to do the signaling. The network speed was at a nominal 8.2 K bits/Sec. The data line uses a 5.00 volts network bias with the BCM as the master module. The BCM communicates with the rest of the modules by toggling the 5.00 volts bias to ground. This system is also address centered. Each network message or frame has a specific address. Once the message is broadcast, it is ignored by all modules except the destination addressed module (s).

NOTE: These early systems marked GM's trend towards the use of ring topology, which they used in successive years. The ring wiring arrangement completes its circuit through the DLC. This is the reason why many GM vehicles carry a jumper at the DLC connector protector cover. If this jumper is left out, the network will continue to operate as long as there is no other network wire breakage. The ring loop can only sustain one breakage.

In this system, a shorted signal line (circuit 800) would bring the network down preventing the BCM from communicating with the rest of the system. An instrument cluster message "Electrical Problem" or "ERROR" would also be generated by this fault. Later model years used two separate networks. One for the more critical modules, like the ECM, ABS and SRS and the other for the so-called Entertainment and Comfort System. In latter years, a bus wiring arrangement was also used in conjunction with the ring. This made for a more difficult system to diagnose and repair.

GM CLASS 2 data bus

In the early 1990's the first of GM's class-2 networked vehicles started to appear. The class-2 network protocol is different than the older UART protocol. The class-2 protocol uses message/node-ID arbitration for its media access and not destination addressed frames, which make it somewhat similar to the CAN protocol. However, the transmitting module address is always transmitted periodically (every 2 seconds) in the state-of-health (SOH) message. This protocol also runs at a much higher speed and uses a ring/bus single wire topology. The bits are formatted as long and short square wave pulses to signify the binary numbers 1 or 0. The bus is held at ground if no modules are communicating.

Any node that starts a communication, does so by sending a series of square-pulses 7.00 volts in amplitude of very short duration (between 60-80 yS). A good data bus diagnostics technique is to disconnect all the modules and connect then one at a time, while trying to establish scanner communications each and every time. When the defective module is connected the scanner will show a no communication with that module. When a star bus configuration is present in the vehicle, the above procedure can be accomplished by disconnecting the main bus connector (network jumper connector) and jumping each of the module data pins to the scanner pin, one at a time .

NOTE: If an oscilloscope is not available use a voltmeter to measure the voltage level of the bus. A normally communicating bus should have between 0.60 and 1.5 volts. If the bus is shorted to ground or voltage then a 0.00 or battery voltage level will be displayed on the meter respectively. This condition may cause the engine not to start and cause a code U1300 or U1301 (bus short to ground or power).

NOTE: The class-2 protocol came about due to tight federal regulations regarding emissions diagnostics. The original implementations of this protocol was for ECM related data only. As time passed, it spread to the rest of the systems. GM generally labeled the class-2 signal wire "circuit 1807".

NOTE: GM kept using a mixture of ring and bus topology on most of their systems, which was a practice acquired during the older UART data line implementation. The different ringto-bus splices are usually imbedded in the fuse box. This is a common cause of trouble for the class-2 network. The ring bus configuration can keep operational in the event that one side of the loop is severed.

The modules on this network are constantly transmitting state of health messages. In the event that one module fails to transmit a SOH message, the other modules will store a loss of SOF message on their internal memory for the faulty module. At key-on start up initialization, each module broadcast its SOH message. An initialization message failure will store a code U1000. An example would be an inoperative IPC (Instrument Panel Cluster) in which case a U type code (network code U1096) would set in the ECM, TCM, ABS and BCM modules. The diagnostics logic in this case is to scan the other modules for a lack of IPC SOH message code. This will prove a faulty IPC on the data bus, as in a defective power or ground circuit for the IPC module. Each SOH message has its unique module identifier (mod-ID).

The module identifier is imbedded inside the particular faulty code. These are some of the more common module identifiers. They are generally consistent but might change slightly from module to module. These codes are always preceded by a U1xxx as in U1096-IPC.

- PCM-096

- BCM-064

- TCM-040

- SDM-088

- EBCM-041

- IPC-096

- HVAC-153

- RADIO-128

- RFA-176

Remember that the U code sets in the other module's memory and not in the faulty module. In this case, the faulty module will not be communicating on the bus and probably inaccessible with the scanner.

NOTE: A very few early models did not set U codes for certain modules. In those cases, an oldfashioned pint-to-point wiring diagnostics approach has to be employed.

The Tech-2 scanner has a dynamic menu configuration feature. At the beginning of the menu options there is also a Message Monitor item, which lists out all the currently communication modules. In order to be on this list, a particular module has to be transmitting a SOH message every two seconds. A faulty module that is not broadcasting a SOH message will not be on the list, which can be confusing to the technician. It is easy to overlook the fact that although a particular module is not present on the list of modules, it might still be installed on the vehicle but simply is not visible. An example would be a faulty ABS module that does not appear on the list although the vehicle is equipped with an ABS system. Since the ABS module is not sending a SOH message, the scanner ignores it and assumes that the vehicle does not have an ABS system. As mentioned before, the proper diagnostic strategy here is to search for a U type code in the other modules' memory, since the other modules are expecting a SOH message from the missing ABS module.

The missing ABS module will generate a "code U1041-no ABS SOH message" on the rest of the modules. Do not rely on the Message Monitor list as the sole indicator of available modules in the system without making an analysis of the rest of the modules' stored faulty U codes.

Doing so can cause confusion by making it look as if the faulty module is not present. Only the modules sending the SOH message will be on the list. Going to the "Tool Option" feature and enabling the Bypass mode can disable the dynamic menu configuration on the Tech-2. In this way, the scanner will list al the possible modules on the vehicle and the faulty module can be manually chosen to communicate with (If possible).

NOTE: The Tech-2's PING-ALL-MODULES menu option is a feature that is used to force all the available modules in a vehicle to broadcast their SOH message. By pinging all modules with the scanner, the display willchange from inactive to active with KOEO.

See our complimentary DVD-Video series for this book.

6. CAN (Controller Area Network)

The Robert Bosch Corporation came up with the initial implementation of the CAN protocol, which was called CAN 1.2. This version allowed for only an 11-bit message identifier (short ID). Therefore, being a fairly small binary number (only 11-bits), the protocol could only distinguish 2050 distinct different messages (ID numbers). Latter on in 1993, a new version was introduced, CAN 2.0 that has the standard 11-bit identifier but also an extended 29-bit identifier mode. This latter version allowed for millions of distinct message combinations, making for a more robust protocol or data exchange agreement rulebook. The hart of the CAN protocol signal is the data frame. The data frame can be looked at as a from of data burst, where the actual sensor/actuator or any other form of data is disassembled or broken into pieces and sent over the network a couple of pieces at a time. These data pieces or fragments travel over the network lines inside data frames and each data frame is separate and distinct from each other. In other words, each data frame has its own identifier and different data fragment inside. As soon as the data frames reach their destination node (specific module (s)), the data fragments are put together again .

The identifier is then discarded and the respective module or modules use the completely reassembled data appropriately. The data frame is composed not only of the two before mentioned pieces (identifier and data), but of many other binary bits that make it possible for all this to work together. In the next part of this article we will be dealing with this information. As a final note of introduction into the CAN protocol, it is important to note that the protocol itself is multi-master. This means that any node at any particular time could access the network and no one node controls the network. Hence the need for specific and distinct identifiers, which reinforces the fact that CAN is a message identifier-oriented protocol.

The CAN protocol has been EPA approved for MY 2003 and up vehicle diagnostics and a legal requirement by the year 2008. This means that the old OBD II SAE J1850 protocol compliant scanner will need some modification in order to communicate using the CAN specification. The main problem is the higher speed of the new CAN network, which is about 10 times faster than the protocols in use today. The new CAN diagnostic systems still use the standard 16 pin OBD II (J1962) connector. However, the new CAN diagnostics data line will be on pins 6 and 14, which before have been manufacturer specific. Future vehicles that are not yet CAN compliant might have these two pins blank. The actual scan tool can be connected to the network either directly or through the gateway circuitry.

The Class C implementation of CAN is called CAN C, which is not to be confused with CAN A or CAN B. These two are actually the CAN protocol's Class A and B implementations. As previously explained, the protocol is separate from the classification. Classification is synonymous with speed and protocol with the data exchange agreement. The CAN A, B and C networks can all be linked via a gateway within the same vehicle, with the actual gateway circuitry imbedded inside a specific module.

The instrument cluster module or the front control module is a good example of a module with imbedded gateway circuitry. It is also worth remembering that the gateway module is not a separate unit, but this circuitry is part of another module's PC board. Another major difference between CAN A and the other CAN implementations is that CAN A runs on only one wire (at much slower speeds) and therefore much cheaper to build. CAN A also uses the vehicle's own ground. While CAN B and C are much faster but run on a two-wire network implementation and do not use the vehicle's ground. The latter types simply use the two network wires for differential signaling. This means that the two data signal voltages are opposite to each other and used for error detection by constantly being compared. In this case, when the signal voltage at one of the CAN data wires go high (CAN H) the other one goes low (CAN L) hence the name differential signaling. Differential signaling is also used for redundancy, in case one of the signal wires shorts out.

Previously, we mentioned that the CAN protocol is a message identifier oriented protocol. Each particular message has what could be considered to be an ID number. Every time this particular node wants to talk, it sends a message ID (identifier) first and then the corresponding data message. If a couple of nodes try to talk at the same time, the node with the highest priority message ID number or identifier wins the right to transmit. This type of identifier arbitration will be explained latter. But, a good example of this is the CAN networked steering angle sensor, which could be considered a high priority sensor and the power seat module. In the event that these two nodes try to send a communications signal at the same time, the steering angle sensor will win the right to the network. This happens simply because the SAS messages are of higher priority than the power seat module. In actuality, the SAS message identifiers have a lower binary number, which translates to higher priority. In other words, the lower the identifier's binary number the higher its priority. As soon as the power seat module sees that there is another node trying to access the network with a higher priority message/lower binary number identifier it simply stops transmission and starts to listen for the particular message.

This also shows that in CAN, the nodes have the ability to both transmit and listen at the same time or CSMA (Carrier Sense Multiple Access) media access method. Carrier meaning the network lines that carry data transmission, sense always listening to the network, multiple access that any node can try and access the network at any time so long as it is idle. In other network protocols, for example, a node can only talk in a specific order so it always has to wait its turn. This is not so with CAN. A CAN node (module or sensor/actuator) can send a multitude of possible different messages and those with the highest priority will always win. The important fact to understand is that each identifier number is message oriented and independent of whatever node/module transmits it. For example, the ECM may have may parameters (messages) to transmit over the network—some of those parameters (messages) will be of high priority (throttle signal, engine speed, etc) and some will be of low priority (A/C compressor switch, battery temperature, etc). The message containing the "engine speed" data will win network access over the message containing the battery temperature data, even though both data frames came from the ECM.

As a final note, an introduction will be made to a somewhat different media access method called Time Division Multiple Access. This media access scheme uses fixed time slots exclusively reserved for every node according to a fixed time schedule. This system does not use a master node to control access but simply allows a predetermined amount of access time to each and every node. The main requirement for this system is a very high synchronization of the oscillator, also called system clock. The system clock is derived from an oscillator and synchronized to each node in the network. The master time-keeper-node or controller is in charge of maintaining a stable clock frequency. The time-keeper-node therefore sends a synchronization message at the right time (according to its internal oscillator) to all nodes so that each node can synch to it. The number of nodes, different messages and the transmission bit rate of the network determines the latency time (delay). Examples of TDMA are systems used in very secured situations such as X-by-wire systems. In X-by-wire, an extreme amount of determinism and security is needed. In these situations, for example, the Pedal Position Sensor or the Brake Pressure Sensor can not wait too long for any other sensor to finish its transmission. By using TDMA the system simply already knows the amount of nodes, messages and network speed (bit rate).

This means that the latency time (hold time while waiting for the transmitting node to finish) is already calculated, since each node has a specific predetermined access time.

Examples of TDMA system protocols are Byteflight, Flexray, and Time-triggered CAN or TTCAN. The Byteflight and Flexray protocols now partly under development could very well mean the future of high speed communications and possible substitutions to the CAN protocol. TTCAN however is simply the CAN protocol implementation of TDMA, since this protocol easily lends itself to time triggered applications. In TTCAN all nodes are synchronized to a synchronization signal pulse at the beginning of each transmission frame.

Each node then can access the network in the same way as in regular CAN. The higher the node's message binary identifier the lower the media access priority and the longer the node has to wait for access. In other words CAN and TDMA can survive together in a highly secured reliable high-speed network.

Finally we come to the heart of the CAN protocol, which is the data frame, but first a brief overview.

• The CAN protocol is based on a linear topology with the number of nodes not specified by the protocol.

• The maximum number of nodes is dictated by the actual hardware being used.

• The maximum length of the network is a function of the data rate or the speed of the network. The faster the network the shorter it has to be and vise-versa.

• CAN networks may use one or two wires for the actual signaling. In class B and C two wires are used.

• CAN is based on message identifiers media access and not node addressing. Whenever a data frame in transmitted, all the nodes receive it. Then, the nodes decide whether the data is relevant to them or not.

• The message identifiers also dictate the level of their priority. This says that high priority messages can access the bus relatively fast, which makes for very short access time latency.

• CAN is a multi-master protocol. No single node controls the bus. Any node can start transmitting as soon as the bus becomes idle.

If multiple nodes try and access the bus at the same time, the node with the higher priority identifier wins access.

• CAN uses collision avoidance bus-access (CSMA/CA). Due to the nature of the CAN bus access scheme, no data frame is lost during bus arbitration.

• The CAN protocol has a short data segment of only 8 bytes. This is sufficient for automotive communications systems. In the event that very long data streams are transmitted, as in re-programming a module, the long data stream is divided into many consecutive data segments. The short data segment enables the CAN protocol to work in extremely adverse condition of electromagnetic interference while guaranteeing very short latency times. In the event of an EMI data frame corruption only the corrupted frame is retransmitted and not the whole data stream.

• CAN has excellent error detection capabilities. Any detected errors lead to an automatic retransmission of the data frame.

• CAN uses deactivation of faulty nodes. This feature prevents the faulty node from constantly disturbing the network traffic.

• CAN is a standardized protocol (Internationally). This allows for decentralized hardware manufacturing, which means that different computer makers can cater to different vehicle manufacturers. Therefore, vehicle manufacturers can buy from different sources thereby lowering costs. The bit frame is the center of the actual CAN transmission. The CAN protocol recognizes four types of bit frames.

• Through the data frame, a node transmits data to all the nodes that want to listen.

• Any network node that wants to request data from another node uses the remote frame.

• The error frame is used by all nodes to identify a transmission error and signals all the nodes to ignore the faulty frame.

• The overload frame is used to cause a delay between frames whenever a transmission delay is needed. Data communications in a CAN network can have either of two states or voltage levels, recessive (high) or dominant (low). A bit level 0=dominant and a bit level 1=recessive. The bus voltage level is always at a recessive level (high) when none of the nodes are transmitting or pulling it down (dominant/low). If we were using a 5 volts bus signal level, then an idle bus level would be at 5 volts or recessive level.

On the other hand, a dominant bus level would be at 0.00 volts, which indicates that a node or multiple nodes are transmitting. The nodes on the network simply toggle or pull the bus voltage level to ground, whenever they start transmitting. The signaling of course happens very fast.

In case of the CAN protocol, at a theoretical maximum of 1 M bit/sec or a practical 500K bit/sec. The recessive bus voltage level is provided by one of the modules in the network and is generally called the bus-bias voltage. Any one of the network modules or nodes can be used to provide the bus-bias voltage level at idle. It is also important to understand that if the biasing module goes down the entire network might also go down unless a backup bias module has been designed into the system. A CAN network can also be implemented in a fiber optic medium. With fiber optics, the recessive and dominant bits can be signaled by bright and dark bus states respectively with the added bonus that the network would be a lot faster. Optical signaling has a much faster data rate.

The CAN bus-access arbitration is based on message identifier priority and the recessive and dominant bus levels are the key to arbitration. A node's starting frame transmission always starts by a dominant bit. This is called the start-of-frame (SOF) bit. At the start of a transmission, any node that has data starts to transmit. At this point, one or multiple nodes can start transmitting at the same time. Right after the SOF bit, the arbitration bits (identifier) are sent. During this arbitration process, all the nodes monitor the bus level and compare it to the level that was just transmitted. Any node that transmitted a recessive bit and monitors a dominant bit stops transmitting and becomes a listener. This is the essence of CSMA (Carrier Sense Multiple Access) media access. The node with the lower binary identifier, then, becomes the network master or the only transmitting node. This node will control media access for the remainder of the transmission frame. As stated before, the lower the message identifier's binary-value the higher the access priority.

This bit arbitration guarantees that only one node can transmit on the bus at a time—in the event that multiple nodes try to access the bus at the same time. Since the node that monitors a bus value that is different than the one was just transmitted stops transmitting, this type of arbitration is called non-destructive. Since this is an arbitration principle of comparing the bus level to the transmitted bit (CSMA/CA), the maximum signal propagation time and the internal node delay time have to be taken into account during design. The maximum network length is limited at any given data rate (speed).

Therefore, the faster the network the shorter it has to be and vise-versa. In other words, in a 50 node CAN network if node 1 switches the network bias voltage dominant (low), it takes that signal some time to travel through the network cable to reach node 50, which is the farthest. This is the signal propagation time and it can not exceed a predetermined time value. Although we are only talking about a couple of microseconds, it does count.

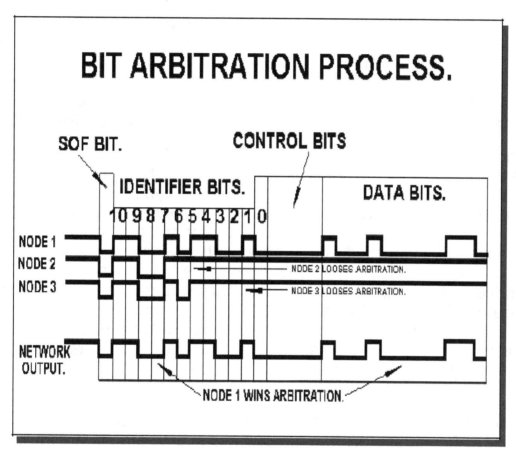

Fig 5. Arbitration process. The signal sequence (identifier) with the lower binary number has the highest frame priority.

There are two different frame formats specified by the CAN protocol, the base format (11-bit identifier) and the extended format (29-bit identifier). The base format is limited in the amount of identifiers available. The extended format allows for a far greater amount of different identifiers to be used. The bit frames are separated from each other by three bit-time recessive bus level. The data frame construction is explained next. Because of space concerns, only the data frame is taken into account which is enough for the automotive repair. A more detailed analysis would fall beyond the scope of this book.

The data frame consists of the SOF (start-of-frame) bit, arbitration bits (identifier), control bits, data bytes (8 bytes), CRC bits, delimiter bit, acknowledgement bit, 2nd delimiter bit and the EOF (end-of-frame) bits, 3 separator bits and then the next frame starts again. A good understanding of frame construction is important for the analysis of network node conflicts. Following are the detailed frame sections definitions.

• The start-of-frame bit is broadcast by the transmitting node and is always dominant (low). All the nodes in the network synchronize to the leading edge of this bit. This bit signals all the nodes that a transmission is about to happen. Multiple nodes can transmit this bit at the same time or synchronize to it. It is only in the next part of the frame where the multiple access conflict can be resolved. See Fig 3.

• The arbitration bits (identifier) are made up of the actual identifier bits and the RTR bit (remote transmission request) bit. It is here where all arbitration conflicts are resolved through identifier priority, either by using the base or extended format. The base format has an 11-bit identifier that allows for 2050 different and distinguishable messages. The extended format on the other hand consists of a 29-bit identifier that allows for over 500 million different messages. The identifier, whether base or extended, is followed by the RTR bit, which indicates whether the frame has the actual data or a request for data. Logically the data has priority over a data request, therefore, the RTR bit is dominant (low) if the frame consists of the actual data and recessive (high) if it is a request for the data.

• The control bits are a series of six bits that indicate such parameters as the length of the frame, distinguishing bits between base or extended format and the number of bytes in the data bit stream.

• The data bits are the actual data to be transmitted and the whole purpose of all this complication. CAN specifies a maximum of 8 bytes.

• The CRC bits are an error checking bit stream and consist of a 15-bit error checking sequence. This allows the node (s) to identify possibly corrupted data. The CRC bits are used in accordance to a complicated mathematical formula that is beyond the scope of the automotive technician's needs.

• The different network nodes use the acknowledgement bit with two delimiter bits at each side to acknowledge the correct reception of a message. In other words, once a node transmits a data frame it expects at least one positive reception acknowledgment from another node.

• The EOF (end-of-frame) bits are used to signal the end of a frame and are a series of seven bits. If all the EOF bits plus the last delimiter bit are recessive then the frame is presumed to be error free. By using frames, the CAN protocol disassembles the data, encodes it and sends it over the network lines. The received data on the other side is decoded, reassembled and used by the receiver node. Long data streams are broken down into smaller parts and subdivided into frames. Those parts are later put back together. Such is the case in reprogramming modules, where long data streams are needed to fully replace the module's software.

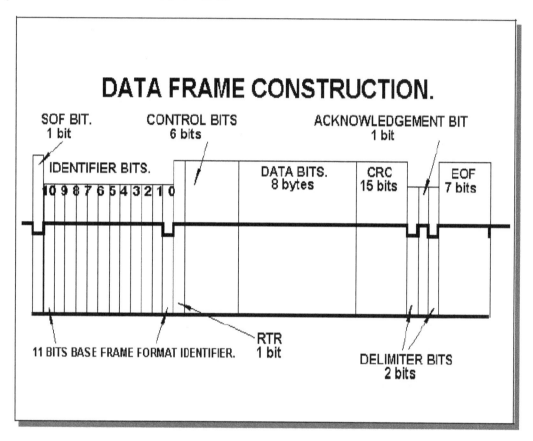

Fig 6. Construction of a Data-Frame.

About the Author:

Mandy Concepcion has worked in the automotive field for over 21 years. He holds a Degree in Applied Electronics Engineering as well as an ASE Master & L1 certification. For the past 16 years he has been exclusively involved in the diagnosis of all the different electronic systems found in today's vehicles. It is here where he draws extensive practical knowledge from his experience and hopes to convey it in his books. Mandy also designs and builds his own diagnostic equipment, DVD-Videos and repair software.